London
Big Ben

London
Big Ben

BY SHERI TAN

INCREDIBUILDS

San Rafael, California

INTRODUCTION

England's capital city of London is brimming with memorable attractions—Buckingham Palace, the London Eye, double-decker buses, and more—but the city's most iconic landmark is undoubtedly Big Ben. People travel from all over the world to visit it. The largest four-faced chiming clock in the world first began to chime in July 1859.

Big Ben is commonly referred to as the clock and the tower that stands at the north end of the Palace of Westminster (better known as the Houses of Parliament). But Big Ben is technically the nickname of the Great Bell inside the clock tower that chimes at the top of every hour.

It is said that Big Ben got its name from Sir Benjamin Hall, the Commissioner of Works, who oversaw the rebuilding of the Palace of Westminster. His name is inscribed on the bell. However, others believe that the name came from Benjamin Caunt, a heavyweight boxing champion of the time, whose nickname was Big Ben.

> "When a man is tired of London, he is tired of life; for there is in London all that life can afford."
>
> –SAMUEL JOHNSON

London has stood along the River Thames since the Romans settled the area about two thousand years ago. Today, 8.2 million people reside in Greater London, and it is easily one of the most diverse cities in the world, with 300 languages spoken! London's cosmopolitan culture is one of the many sources of the city's vibrant atmosphere; the multicultural hub also features a rich history, strong support of the arts, numerous museums, and a well-connected underground rail system.

THE CLOCK

The official name of Big Ben's clock is the Great Clock of Westminster.

At the base of each clock face is the Latin inscription *Domine salvam fac Reginam nostram Victoriam Primam,* which means "O Lord keep safe our Queen Victoria the First."

BY THE NUMBERS:

23 feet	Diameter of clock face
14 feet	Length of minute hand
9 feet	Length of hour hand
2 feet	Height of each numeral on the clock face
312 pieces	Number of glass pieces on each clock face

BUILDING THE CLOCK

While the Palace of Westminster was being rebuilt after a fire destroyed it in 1834, Parliament decided that a clock tower should be included in the design. The architect, Sir Charles Barry, called for input from the Astronomer Royal, George Airy, who said that "the Great Clock should be so accurate that the first strike for each hour shall be accurate to within one second of time."

Airy enlisted the expertise of clockmaker Edmund Beckett Denison to help him realize his vision. Denison came up with a novel way to ensure the accuracy of the clock, and in 1852, Edward John Dent was chosen to build it. But, he passed away a year later, leaving his stepson, Frederick Rippon Dent, to finally complete the project.

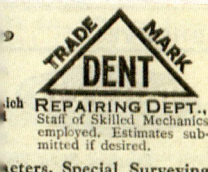

THE TOWER

Standing 315 feet high, the tower that houses the clock and bell was designed by Augustus Pugin in Gothic Revival style as part of the new Palace of Westminster. It was called simply the Clock Tower until 2012, when it was officially renamed the Queen Elizabeth II Tower to celebrate the Diamond Jubilee of Queen Elizabeth II.

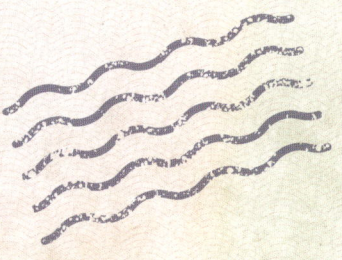

It's true!
The tower leans . . .
Ever since excavation work was done on a nearby tunnel, the Elizabeth Tower has tilted about 9 inches northwest.

BUILDING THE BELL

The Great Bell in use today is actually the second bell that was made for the clock tower. The original bell was a 14.5-tonne bell cast in 1856 by Warner's Foundry in Stockton-on-Tees, but it cracked during testing.

The second bell, cast at the Whitechapel Bell Foundry in 1858, weighed 13.8 tonnes. Standing seven feet two inches tall, this new bell was made of tin and copper and included pieces of the original bell. Oddly enough, the second bell also cracked! It happened about two months after it first chimed in 1859. But it appeared too difficult a task to remove the bell to repair it, so the crack is still there. The decision was made to rotate the bell a quarter turn clockwise and strike it with a lighter hammer. So the bell makes a less-than-perfect but still distinct tone.

The bell is rung not with a clapper on the inside, but with a hammer that strikes the outside of the bell.

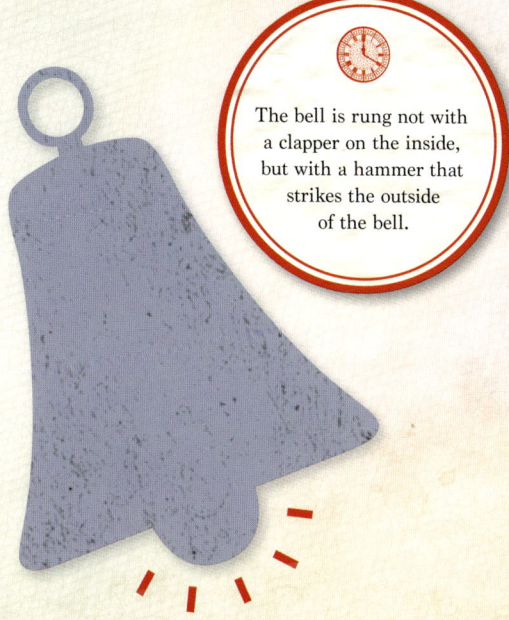

The bell is rung not with a clapper on the inside, but with a hammer that strikes the outside of the bell.

THE CHIMES OF BIG BEN

The Great Bell rings at the top of the hour. There are four smaller bells that surround the Great Bell, and they ring at each quarter hour. The set of quarter bells includes a G#, F#, E, and B. Together, across the hour, these bells play a tune called "Westminster Quarters," which is now used in churches all over England.

SILENCE OF THE CHIMES

There have been several times during Big Ben's history when it stopped chiming, including:

- Two years during World War I, to avoid attack by German zeppelins. The clock faces were also not lit.
- New Year's Eve 1962, when the cold weather froze the hands of the clock, so the new year was rung in ten minutes late!
- January 30, 1965, for the funeral of Winston Churchill.
- April 17, 2013, for the funeral of Margaret Thatcher.
- Starting in 2017, for an estimated four years of restoration work, with exceptions for major events such as New Year's Eve and Remembrance Day.

> "It was a few minutes before the eleventh hour of the eleventh day of the eleventh month. I stood at the window of my room looking up Northumberland Avenue towards Trafalgar Square, waiting for Big Ben to tell that the War was over."
>
> —*WINSTON CHURCHILL*, November 11, 1918, at the end of World War I, *WINSTON S. CHURCHILL: WORLD IN TORMENT, 1916–1922 (VOLUME IV)*, by Sir Martin Gilbert

While London's residents and visitors have seen and heard Big Ben in person, the bell's fame has spread far and wide with appearances not only in books and films, but also in TV and video games!

Big Ben has appeared in:

- *Mrs. Dalloway*, Virginia Woolf (book, 1925)
- *Peter Pan* (film, 1953)
- *Mary Poppins* (film, 1964)
- *The 39 Steps* (film, 1978)
- *The Simpsons*, "Lisa's Wedding" (TV, 1995)
- *SimCity 4* (computer game, 2003)
- *Doctor Who*, "Aliens of London" (TV, 2005)
- *Assassin's Creed Syndicate* (video game, 2015)
- . . . and many more!

Big Ben's chimes also make an appearance in music—in the opening of *A London Symphony* by Ralph Vaughan Williams.

FOR ALL TIME

Big Ben started keeping time in May 1859 and has functioned steadily since the reign of Queen Victoria. For many Britons, it is not just a bell or a clock or a clock tower but a symbol of British pride and resilience. For visitors, no trip is complete without seeing—and hearing—firsthand this engineering marvel that connects them with a part of British heritage and history. Indeed, Big Ben continues to be as culturally important to England and the world as it was when it was first built.

MAKE IT YOUR OWN

One of the great things about IncrediBuilds™ models is that each one is completely customizable. The untreated natural wood can be decorated with paints, pencils, pens, beads, sequins—the list goes on and on!

Before you start building and decorating your model, choose a theme and make a plan. You can create a replica of the iconic Big Ben, or you can make something completely different. Anything goes! Read through these sample projects to get you started and those creative juices flowing.

DAYTIME

1. Paint the rooftops gray.
2. Paint the sides of the building and the tower sides light tan.
3. Paint the base light gray.
4. Paint all the window and engraved details in medium brown.
5. Paint the windows on the tower roof dark gray with light tan for the overhangs.
6. Paint the clock face white.
7. Add the clock hands and details with black paint.

NIGHTTIME

1. Paint the rooftops dark brown.
2. Paint the sides of the main building and the bottom third of the clock tower yellow.
3. Paint the small tower and the mid-section of the clock tower orange-brown.
4. Paint the top section of the clock tower medium brown. Use a damp brush to blend the edges of each color section together to create a gradient.
5. Use orange-brown to follow the engravings and add detail to the yellow painted sections.

6. Use dark brown to follow the engravings and add detail to the medium brown painted sections.

7. Paint the clock face white and add the details in black.

8. Paint the rim above the clock face in a lime green.

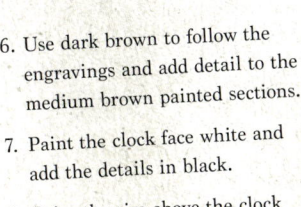

A Division of Insight Editions
PO Box 3088
San Rafael, CA 94912
www.insighteditions.com
www.incredibuilds.com

Find us on Facebook: www.facebook.com/InsightEditions
Follow us on Twitter: @insighteditions

All rights reserved. Published in 2018 by Insight Editions, San Rafael, California. No part of this book may be reproduced in any form without written permission from the publisher.

Copyright © 2018 by Insight Editions

ISBN: 978-1-68298-188-7

Publisher: Raoul Goff
Associate Publisher: Vanessa Lopez
Art Director: Chrissy Kwasnik
Designer: Lauren Chang
Editor: Rebekah Piatte
Editorial Assistant: Holly Fisher
Production Editor: Lauren LePera
Production Director: Lina s Palma
Product Development Manager: Rebekah Piatte
Model Designer: HeJian Zhu, TeamGreen
Craft Samples: Jill Turney

Photo Credits
Page 1: AVA Bitter/shutterstock.com
Pages 2–3: Pajor Pawel/shutterstock.com
Page 4: Danussa/shutterstock.com
Page 7: bioraven/shutterstock.com
Page 8: Jacek Wojnarowski/shutterstock.com
Page 13: Hal_P/shutterstock.com
Page 17: cristapper/shutterstock.com
Page 19: Alexey Fedorenko/shutterstock.com
Pages 20–21: Dana.S/shutterstock.com
Page 23: Mohana Anton Meryl/shutterstock.com
Page 25: Ivan Mateev/shutterstock.com
Page 26: S. Borisov/shutterstock.com
Instructions: Pajor Pawel/shutterstock.com

Insight Editions, in association with Roots of Peace, will plant two trees for each tree used in the manufacturing of this book. Roots of Peace is an internationally renowned humanitarian organization dedicated to eradicating land mines worldwide and coverting war-torn lands into productive farm and wildlife habitats. Roots of Peace will plant two million fruit and nut trees in Afghanistan and provide farmers there with the skills and support necessary for sustainable land use.

Manufactured in China

10 9 8 7 6 5 4 3 2 1